Spider Lilies

The Rocky Shoals Spider Lilies of Landsford Canal State Park
A Natural History Landmark of the Catawba River Valley

By The Katawba Valley Land Trust
Photographs by Bill Price

Partners in the Creation of this Book

In addition to the Katawba Valley Land Trust, the following organizations were major partners in the creation of this book:

S.C. Department of Parks, Recreation & Tourism: The PRT staff manages and protects the wonderful resources of Landsford Canal State Park, including the spider lilies, and makes them compatibly available for the public to enjoy. Their staff was a major contributor to this book.

Duke Energy: This book was made possible through a $5,000 contribution from Duke Energy to the Katawba Valley Land Trust. The gift is an example of Duke Energy's continued support of the protection of this stretch of the Catawba River. In 1970, the company donated approximately 200 acres along the western shore of the river in Chester County to the people of South Carolina. The land featured the remains of the historic Landsford Canal and was soon dedicated as Landsford Canal State Park.

S.C. Department of Natural Resources: The department supported the development of this book and participated in the expansion of public lands at Landsford through a federal Forest Legacy Program. DNR now manages over 1,000 acres adjacent to Landsford Canal State Park.

Crescent Resources: This subsidiary of Duke Energy has cooperated with public and private natural resource agencies to add significantly to the land which is protected in the Landsford area, providing signicant buffers for the population of spider lilies.

Dupont of Camden/Invista, South Carolina: Dupont contributed $1,000 to the Katawba Valley Land Trust to help provide for the completion of this book.

The Garden Club of South Carolina, Inc.: The Garden Club contributed $1,000 to the Katawba Valley Land Trust to help provide completion of this book.

Palmetto Conservation Foundation: This state-wide public interest group has provided valuable assistance in the publication of this book. PCF is a non-profit membership organization dedicated to conserving South Carolina's natural resources.

Published by: Palmetto Conservation Foundation/PCF Press, 1314 Lincoln St., Suite 305, Columbia, SC 29201-3154 www.palmettoconservation.org

10 09 08 07 06 05 04 03 02 01

Printed in China by C & C Offset Printing Co., LTD.

Library of Congress Cataloging-in-Publication Data

Spider lilies : the Rocky Shoals spider lilies of Lansford Canal State Park : a natural landmark of the Catawba River Valley / text by Katawba Valley Land Trust ; photos by Bill Price.
    p. cm.
 Includes bibliographical references.
 ISBN 0-9745284-6-3 (alk. paper)
 1. Hymenocallis caroliniana--South Carolina--Lansford Canal State Park. 2. Lansford Canal State Park (S.C.) I. Katawba Valley Land Trust. II. Price, Bill.
 QK495.A484S65 2006
 584'.34--dc22
                  2006022996

Our Katawba Valley Land Trust hopes that you will enjoy this publication about the Rocky Shoals Spider Lily. We as a people are most fortunate to have the exquisite beauty of this native wild plant in our Catawba River for all our citizens to enjoy and to reflect upon the silent beauty of our natural world. Only God can create a wild plant like our lily, and once it becomes extinct man cannot bring it back.

I have often thought about our Carolina hero, William Richardson Davie of Revolutionary War fame, and his thoughts as he viewed, in late May of the early 1800s, the Queen of the Catawba River Valley, our Landsford Shoals Spider Lily. The Chester County side of the Catawba River at Landsford was Davie's soil, his land, his Tivoli Plantation. Davie could have only marveled at the wonder of it all, the fragrance and beauty of Hymenocalis Coronaria: Our Lily!

Over the last eleven years our Katawba Valley Land Trust has been involved in 35 projects of land conservation plus a number of community projects such as this lily book.

We appreciate the many individuals, corporations, and state agencies that have continually given the Katawba Valley Land Trust encouragement and the needed support to continue our mission of the protection of South Carolina's natural resources, open lands, waters, vistas and local history.

How fortunate we are to have Landsford Canal State Park as a platform to view the Rocky Shoal;s Spider Lily as well as to enjoy the abundant wildlife beauty of the Catawba River.

A special word of appreciation to Duke Energy Corporation for their special gift to publish this book and to our lily resource team who, through their individual and collective efforts, made this publication possible.

We invite you to join the Katawba Valley Land Trust and to travel with our Trust as we continue our land conservation journey.

Katawba Valley Land Trust President
D. Lindsay Pettus

The following individuals and representatives came together as a team to plan and prepare this book.

Dick Christie, S.C. Department of Natural Resources (DNR)

Larry Davenport, Samford University

John Garton, Katawba Valley Land Trust (KVLT) and S.C. Wildlife Federation

Jen Huff, Duke Energy

Al James, S.C. Department of Parks, Recreation & Tourism (PRT)

Don Oneppo, PRT

Lindsay Pettus, KVLT

Irvin Pitts, PRT

Jane and George Polk, S.C. Sierra Club

Susan Jones Ferguson, Jones Ferguson Graphic Design

Bill Price, Bill Price Photography

Malcom Schaffer, Devine, Tarbell & Associates, Inc.

Robert Siler, KVLT

Jim Sorrow, DNR

Jason Walls, Duke Energy

Paul Gettys, KVLT

Ken Driggers, Palmetto Conservation Foundation

Table of Contents

F o r e w o r d

Over the years my travels with the SCETV program "Nature Scene" took me and the production crew to many wonderful settings. We did programs in all 50 states and beyond. Every place we visited was special, but my favorite place has always been my home state of South Carolina. Even though it is the smallest Southeastern state, it contains a great variety of habitats, or homes, for plants and animals. South Carolina has everything from the Blue Ridge mountains to the Atlantic Ocean, with Piedmont, Sandhills and the Coastal Plain in between.

One of the unique habitats found on the Piedmont is the rocky shoals habitat known as the Catawba River rapids at Landsford Canal State Park. These rapids, or shoals, and the abundant wildlife that utilize them are a special treat anytime of the year. However, when their most famous inhabitant the Rocky Shoals Spider Lily is in bloom, they provide one of the grandest natural history sights in the southeastern United States. This book, by the Katawba Valley Land Trust and their partners, provides information about the life history of these marvelous spider lilies, their ecological associations and their home.

The major goal of "Nature Scene" was to connect humans with nature: to help them become more aware of the natural world in ways that would enrich their lives. I know that this book, with its beautiful photos and sketches, will help many of its readers connect with this special place. I encourage you to read this book, share it with someone else and visit Landsford Canal State Park for yourself. Mark on your calendar the next Lily Fest and be sure to attend. Then let the sights and sounds of the rapids, with their sea of Spider Lilies in full bloom, connect you with the Catawba River and all of its resources that both enrich and sustain our lives.

Rudy Mancke

Background

In recent years, our regional communities have become more aware of the Catawba River and its value to our people. We are gaining a better recognition of the river's importance to the sustainability of our daily lives, and of its beauty, its wildlife and its wildflower inhabitants. This has come about in part due to a series of constructive planning and action processes that have worked to bring the river, as well as its natural and cultural resources to the attention of regional leaders, educators and other decision makers.

Some of these processes and actions and their respective teams include the following:

Catawba River Corridor Task Force - A community-based initiative of York, Chester and Lancaster counties.

PRT and DNR - state agencies that jointly produced the Catawba River Corridor Plan in 1994. This plan has been the basis of many sound planning decisions along the river in recent years. They are also working cooperatively along the Catawba River and, with the assistance of conservation groups, having great successes in raising public awareness in land and water conservation.

Catawba River Implementation Committee - A committee of about twenty local citizens that was created by the Corridor Task Force to help implement its plan. The committee meets monthly in Rock Hill to learn about plans associated with the river and to work to make activities compatible with good resource conservation.

Katawba Valley Land Trust and Nation Ford Land Trust - Two private land trusts, created in the early 1990's, have provided the means for significant successes in land conservation along the Catawba River in recent years.

Great Falls Hometown Association - a group working toward sound resource planning in the Great Falls area. GFHA is developing plans for their area based on the natural and cultural resources of the river.

Landsford Canal State Park - a centerpiece of the Catawba River Corridor Plan that, as a result of the cooperative actions of the above groups, has grown from 210 acres in the mid-1990's to more than 1,400 acres today.

Buffer Ordinances - both Chester and York counties have created ordinances that provide for natural buffer strips along the shores of the Catawba River and its major tributaries, helping to protect water quality and wildlife habitat in these important locations. In addition, Crescent Resources, LLC of Charlotte has agreed to place permanent conservation easements on all its holdings along the free-flowing river and all river tributaries as they sell these properties. The company also has a program to assist other riverside owners to establish such conservation easements.

Lily Fest - the one-day annual celebration of the spider lilies at Landsford Canal State Park has grown from being attended by a few hundred visitors to several thousand visitors. It is a major annual date for the public to connect with their river and is discussed in some detail in this book.

Bi-State Catawba River Task Force (BSCRTF) - a group involving more than thirty different organizations from both North and South Carolina provides a forum for discussing issues affecting the Catawba River.

"The scenery here cannot fail to interest. Ten thousand rocks and grassy islet meet the traveler's eye, ten thousand murmuring streams meander through them."

Robert Mills

Architect and designer of the Landsford Canal and the Washington Monument describing the Landsford areas in his statistics of South Carolina, 1826.

Introduction

Each year on a Sunday in May, Landsford Canal State Park hosts "Lily Fest." This one-day event celebrates the Rocky Shoals Spider Lilies that grow in the rapids at the historic river crossing, "Land's Ford." This annual cycle of the spider lilies is truly an item worthy of celebration. Beginning in mid-May, this rare and spectacular plant flowers in grand profusion across the width of the Catawba River rapids, producing what has rightly been called "one of the grandest natural history sights in the southeastern US."

The "spider-like" flowers are large showy blossoms perched on 30-inch tall plants. They fill the expansive river shoals with a dazzling display of color that invariably produces an exclamation of awe from people seeing them at their peak for the first time. But many of the visitors at Lily Fest are not first timers - rather, they have been here before, some many times. And each year they come back and gather at the river bank with grandparents, parents, children, and grandchildren to see the spider lilies, to hear the river rush over its rocky bed, and to marvel at the unique setting.

The spider lilies at Landsford Canal are not only very special in themselves, but they also serve as grand ambassadors of the Catawba River and its other natural resources. Many people have grown up near the river but never thought of it as something truly special. Rather, it has simply been something they "drive across" during a busy day's schedule.

That is, until they experience the spider lilies in bloom at Landsford. Then, for many, the river takes on a more special quality - it becomes something to appreciate, to feel good about, even to cherish. This personal discovery of the spider lilies often leads to further awareness that the river provides homes for eagles, diverse aquatic life, and splendid scenery, while also serving many of our human societal needs. With this awareness comes realization that the river is a part of our community and something that connects us to each other, to our past, and to the natural resources that sustain us. Most importantly, getting to know the spider lilies can readily lead to an awareness of the fact that - while we will continue to need the river to serve our societal needs - we also now want that service to be accomplished in ways that are compatible with eagles, aquatic life, and spider lilies.

This booklet tells the story of the spider lilies that live in the Catawba River at Landsford Canal State Park. We hope it makes these flowers, and subsequently their river, better known to the public, especially to today's youth and students. It is they who, in the future, will have to make decisions about the river, its spider lilies, and all the other forms of life that the river sustains.

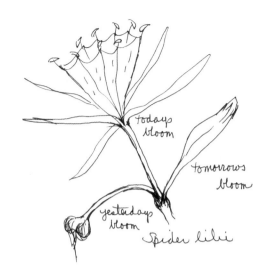

The Rocky Shoals Spider Lily

The Plant

The Rocky Shoals Spider Lily is a member of the plant family Amaryllidaceae - which is the Amaryllis or Daffodil family. This group of plants is characterized as bulbed plants that have long, narrow leaves with six parted flowers. The flowers are showy and certainly rather "lily like" in appearance, but the members of the amaryllis family are not true lilies. (True lilies are in the plant family Liliaceae.) Some other native wildflowers of the Carolinas that belong to the Amaryllis family are the atamasco lily and yellow stargrass. A very familiar non-native member of the family is the daffodil, which is abundantly planted in yards and has escaped to country roadsides.

The scientific name of the Rocky Shoals Spider Lily is Hymenocallis coronaria. The first word in this name is the genus of the plant (of which there are several species), while the second name refers to this particular species. Its scientific name means "the beautiful crown-like membrane" and refers to the corona-like structure that supports the flower's pollen bearing structures.

There are a couple of other spider lily species in South Carolina that are generally similar in appearance to the Rocky Shoals Spider Lily. However, these other species can live and reproduce in swamp forests and along stream banks, and do not live in the unique rocky shoals habitat where Hymenocallis coronaria occurs. None of these other species form the expansive and beautiful flowering colonies that are formed by the Rocky Shoals Spider Lily.

Rocky Shoals Spider Lilies are herbaceous perennials, meaning that the plant has no woody stems and that new leaves grow from established rootstock each year. The leaves and flower stems arise from bulbs which are attached to rocky substrates in the shallow waters of river shoals (or rapids). This harsh habitat dominated by full sun, rocks, and rushing water, is the only habitat utilized by the Rocky Shoals Spider Lily throughout its natural range.

From its rocky attachment, each mature bulb produces a series of 6 to 10 green leaves that emerge about 30 inches above the water. The leaves are up to 2 inches wide, and uniform green in color. A separate stem that will support 6-8 flower buds arises among the leaves. These flower buds will open, one at a time, during the late spring flowering season. It is these flowers that produce the "natural show" that is the highlight of the annual Lily Fest. But, to understand all that goes into providing for one of these mature plants, let's start at the beginning.

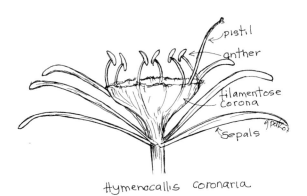

pistil
anther
filamentose
corona
Sepals
9 Dec03

Hymenocallis coronaria

Reproduction

The spider lily flowers are approximately 3 inches wide. Their structure begins as a narrow floral tube that expands upward into a very dazzling and distinctly shaped flower. They are generally pure white in appearance, but contain yellow-green colors in the floral tube. Each flower has six outer parts making up its perianth. These include three petals and three sepals, which are similar in appearance and give the plant its "spidery" nature. (In many plant species, the petals and sepals are distinct from each other, not similar, with the petals being the showy part of the flower.) Toward the center of the flower are its reproductive structures. The six stamens, that support the pollen-bearing anthers, are connected by a filamentous crown (corona). It is this corona, in conjunction with the "spidery" perianth that gives the spider lilies their very distinct and showy appearance. Emerging from within the circular corona is the pistil which contains the ovary at its base, and which will form the seed to produce future spider lilies.

Pollination

A major function of flowers is to produce seed which helps insure continuation of the species and helps the species spread to new areas of suitable habitat. Studies on the reproductive biology of the spider lily in Alabama have been conducted by Dr. Larry Davenport and Dr. Randy Haddock. They have observed sphinx moths (hawk moths) visiting the flowers after dark and consider them to be at least one of the likely pollinators of the spider lilies. They have also observed pipevine swallowtail butterflies visiting the flowers. In the rapids at Landsford we have observed sphinx moths, as

well as various species of bees and flies, visiting the flowers. Many of these are evening visitors, for it is toward sundown that the Rocky Shoals Spider Lily sets its table for pollinators.

At Landsford, our observations have shown that a number of different insects visit the newly opened spider lily flowers prior to darkness. These include various species of bees and flies. After dark, we have also observed sphinx moths visiting the flowers for nectar, as have Drs. Davenport and Haddock in Alabama. We have been unable to capture a sphinx moth to determine the species that we are observing, but in Alabama the researchers have recorded the plebian sphinx moth (Paratrea plebeja) as a visitor to the spider lilies. The reproductive biology of the Rocky Shoals Spider Lily is just one of the subjects associated with this plant that is worthy of further study.

Reproduction from Seeds

New plants can originate late each summer from seeds. Mature seeds are dropped from established plants and land in the water. The seeds sink to the bottom of the river within the shallow rapids and begin the risky business of "trying" to establish new spider lily plants. Their success depends upon their coming to rest in an adequate place where they can "take root," grow, and most importantly, hold their

However, these new seedlings are not yet guaranteed a future in the spider lily colony. Growing in soft, shiftable sand is not a secure footing, by any means, in the ever-changing current conditions of the Catawba River. Unless these seedlings can quickly wrap part of their new root system around a piece of stable bedrock, they are likely to be washed out of their sandy bed during the high river flows that typically occur during winter months. The fate of these young seedlings, probably like most of the seeds that were produced during the previous summer, is to fail to become part of the colony. But, the good news is that this failure is due in large part to the fact that so much of the useable habitat within the shoals is already occupied by healthy, vigorous spider lily plants.

Reproduction from Bulbs

Once a spider lily plant is established in the shoals, it can also reproduce in another manner - by the original bulb producing additional bulbs. Spider lilies are closely related to the non-native daffodil that is so familiar to many of us. If you plant a single daffodil bulb it will produce a single plant the first year. But, after a period of years there will be clusters of leaves and numerous flowers where the single plant originally occurred. If you dig up the original bulb, you would find that there is now a cluster of bulbs. This is the result of the original bulb forming additional bulbs. This same process occurs with spider lilies and allows a newly established seedling plant to grow and to then expand into the available habitat that immediately surrounds it.

position against the ever-changing currents of the river. Two opportunities for this to happen are:

1) Seeds can become wedged into rock crevices where they can immediately "take hold" and resist the changing currents of the river, or
2) They can land in some quiet sandy-bottomed area where the sand is not constantly being shifted by the river currents.

Here in these types of settings, the seeds can begin the process of growing into a mature plant.

For a Rocky Shoals Spider Lily seed to find and utilize these seedbed options is not as convenient and simple as it sounds. First, most of the "good" rock crevices are already inhabited by mature spider lilies. Over many years, the colony has been producing seed and those seeds have found and colonized most of the crevices. So, when today's seeds land in those areas, they find them already occupied, and there is no place to "take root."

However, seeds still have opportunities to flourish. The current moves the seeds further downstream, maybe yet to find an adequate rock crevice or to land in a quiet deposit of sand on the river bottom. If the river current allows the seed to remain on this sand long enough, it will germinate and the leaf of a new seedling will soon emerge above the water surface. By early September, some local areas within the Landsford shoals are dotted with such seedlings, growing from a sandy-bottomed area of the river, and suggesting a future cluster of new plants.

5:30 pm   5:45 pm   6:15 pm

A Day in the Life of the Rocky Shoals Spider Lily

For most people, it is the flower of the Rocky Shoals Spider Lily that is its most notable aspect, the most alluring part of the plant. Without the flowers we would not be drawn to the plant in the numbers that we are; we would not come to the river in late May each year by the thousands to visit the plant and its expansive colony. However, it is not to attract people that the Rocky Shoals Spider Lily puts on its annual flowering show - it intends no business with people. It does have business with another set of visitors who come to its flowers - its insect pollinators. In order to accommodate these visitors, the Rocky Shoals Spider Lily has arranged its annual and daily schedules.

The flowers of the spider lilies open late in the day, and are very much past their peak one day later. When they first open the flowers are at the peak of their fragrance, and it is thus likely that their strategy for pollination is to attract pollinators that are active in the last hours of daylight and into the hours of darkness. The flowers, their delicate coronas, and their abundant pollen on their raised anthers, are all very fragile and showy. When the flowers first open, all of these elements are in peak condition for the evening's and night's work of attracting pollinators. By sunlight the next morning, the flowers that opened the previous evening are past their peak in appearance, and they slowly deteriorate during the day. Each evening's new flowers, when they are opened, are readily distinguished from the previous day's flowers, which have a decidedly more "worn" appearance.

Based on field notes from several evenings spent in the rapids to observe the opening of spider lily flowers, we have these data on portions of the daily cycle of a Rocky Shoals Spider Lily. The following five photographs illustrate the opening of a single flower.

5:00 pm - Thousands of flowers decorate the colony and from some distance they all appear as generally fresh flowers. However, when we examine them closely we can tell that none of them are new flowers, rather they are all one day or more old. "Today's flowers" have not begun to open yet. On the flower stalk of each plant there are a number of un-opened flower buds. The buds are white 1.5 - 2.0 inch tubes that are unopened flowers for coming days. Of the several flower buds on each plant, one is obviously more swollen than the others - this one will be tonight's flower for that particular spider lily plant. We observe a number of these swollen flower buds and begin to take notes.

The first notable activity associated with the open-ing of the swollen flower bud involves the six parts of the perianth (petals), the spidery outer "legs" of the flower. These

6:45 pm   7:45 pm

begin to separate at their distal end and begin to "stretch out." First, one or two of the segments may open, with the others remaining connected. Soon all will be open. These opening actions of the perianth segments are most likely to come in quick bursts, as if reacting to internal pressure.

6:00 - 6:30 pm - The first flowers begin to open. From the first opening activity, individual flowers typically take 10 to 15 minutes to fully open, but this is variable.

The petals do not go to a fully open position immediately, but rather go through a series of intermediate steps, with periods of non-activity being followed by another burst of opening action.

6:30 - 7:00 pm - Many flowers in the colony begin opening.

As the petals open, the inner portions of the flower, the corona with its anthers, also work toward a fully open position.

7:45 pm - The colony's complement of flowers for that night (numbering in the thousands) seems fully open.

The newly opened flowers are truly perfect in appearance. They are a very bright white overall, with a yellow center down inside the interior base of the flower. Each of the six anthers holds robust amounts of bright orange pollen above the rim of the corona.

The odor of the flowers is also very noticeable just after the flowers open, when the colony area is filled with the spider lilies' distinct and pleasant odor. With their flowers' synchronized openings late in the evening, their perfect appearance and abundant odor at this time, it is easy to suspect that this is their time of day to attract specific pollinators to help their process for seed formation.

A Year in the Life of the Rocky Shoals Spider Lily

Some of the major natural features that greet the visitor to the Catawba River Rapids at Landsford Canal State Park are the exposed bedrock of the river bed, the rushing waters of the river, and the protected forests that surround the river. All of these features are stable and seemingly unchanging elements. However, to visit these rapids at different seasons is to get the impression that you are visiting different places - that "this can't be the same place I visited before." The change is dramatic, and brought about by changes in the seasonal aspects of the native plants and animals of the river. Of these, none are so dramatic, nor so dominant a feature of the overall scene, as the seasonal growth and flowering of the Rocky Shoals Spider Lily. First, the lilies turn the scene from gray to green as they leaf out in early spring. Then the world turns white during the peak of lily flowering. Then, in high summer, the rapids are a lush green as the lily leaves reach their peak.

The spider lilies aren't really the dominant factor in this broad natural scene; the river itself is. But, during the warm seasons so much of the river is hidden by the abundance and brightness of a seemingly endless sea of leaves and flowers that, to our human senses, for at least several months of the year, this scene belongs to Hymenocallis coronaria.

What follows is a brief description of what the visitor to the banks of the Catawba River in the immediate area of the spider lily overlook is likely to observe on a seasonal basis.

Winter (December - Mid March)

Go to the riverbank and look out across the rapids on a cloudy overcast day in mid winter and you might feel that you are looking at a black and white photo. The river, its exposed gray-colored bedrock, the white water in the rapids, and the largely leafless trees provide little color. Within the rapids there is no green vegetation.

The spider lilies are dormant, largely leafless, and in little evidence to visitors. If the river flow is high, the spider lilies will not be in evidence at all. If the river is at a low flow you may be able to observe (especially with use of binoculars) some of the bulbs just at the water level. Some bulbs may have short green leaves extending 2-3 inches above the top of the bulbs. Others may have no green showing at all.

Other Winter Features

• *The gleaming white bark of the sycamore trees that occur along the river banks lights up like candles on sunny winter days.*

• *Ring-billed gulls that spent the summer nesting along the Great Lakes (and points north) can be commonly seen over the river.*

• *Great blue herons wade among the river rocks feeding on fish.*

• *Double-crested cormorants actively dive in the rapids during their search for food.*

Early Spring (Mid-March to early May)

Spring arrives in full force across the Piedmont of South Carolina this time of year. At the Landsford rapids, the numerous islets within the river go through a transformation in color from the general gray of winter to the full bright green of summer as black willow trees, water willows, and the Rocky Shoals Spider Lilies send out their leaves for the year.

Spider lily leaves begin to emerge and show rapid growth. If the river flows are high, the growth may not be immediately evident. But when flows are low, the new leaves can be seen projecting just above the bulbs among the bedrock. By May the leaves are reaching their maximum length of 2-3 ft in height, and flowering stalks with their flower buds are appearing. At this time the leaves extend well above the water level, even during normal high river flows.

By May there are seemingly acres of these leaves. But this isn't yet the real show. Those familiar with the spider lilies know that the real show is about to begin!

Other Early Spring Features

• *Riverbank trees leaf out and there is a burst of animal activity.*

• *Within the rapids the beautiful red-winged blackbirds begin nesting and feeding among the new leaves of the lilies. By May, their constant and noisy comings-and-goings are readily observed by visitors.*

• *Beavers and muskrats ply the river late and early in the day.*

• *Harmless water snakes bask on tree branches over the river in the warm spring sunshine.*

• *On mild sunny days, river cooter turtles bask on exposed rocks and logs in the rapids area.*

• *Bald eagles and ospreys hunt in the rapids for food to sustain themselves and the young they are raising in nearby nests.*

Late Spring (Mid-May to Mid-June)

On a sunny day in early May, a visitor to the rapids might notice a few isolated spots of white among the abundant green spider lily leaves that now dominate the rapids area. From the river bank, these distant "white spots" might be mistaken for anything including small pieces of paper that have blown out into the river and gotten caught on spider lily leaves. But a look through binoculars reveals that these "white spots" are really the year's first spider lily blooms.

The opening of these few first blooms is an indication that the peak flowering time is just ahead. Over the next week or so, these few blooms become thousands of blooms. By middle May, the spider lily colony is in peak flowering condition and 3-inch wide, snow white blossoms are open and perched over the flowing river on their 30-inch-high flower stalks. Even though there are many more green leaves than flowers, the overall impression is that the shoals of the river are pure white. It is breath taking. "One of the grandest natural history sights in the southeast US" is in full swing. It is the time for Lily Fest!

Other Late Spring Features

• *In and around the rapids many of the plant and animal activities of early spring are continuing, some in greater abundance than in previous weeks. Overall, this is a season of high animal activity.*

• *Aquatic turtles make their annual trip ashore to dig nests and lay eggs in the soil of the riverbank and its adjacent areas near the river. These turtle species include river cooters, snapping turtles, and musk turtles.*

• *Bright yellow prothonotary warblers (swamp canaries) fly back-and-forth as they bring food to their young in their riverside cavity nests.*

• *Redbreast sunfish, largemouth bass, and other fish species construct their nests in the river and raise their broods in eddies and other quiet water areas within the rapids.*

• *Water willow, the other abundant herbaceous plant species that shares the rapids with the Rocky Shoals Spider Lily.*

Summer (Mid- June through August)

A visit to Landsford during this season rewards the visitor with a sea of green plants in the rapids largely represented by spider lilies and water willows. Although the peak blooming time for the spider lily is finished for the year, a few white blooms can still be seen throughout the colony through August. However the dominant aspect is again, as just before the blooming period, provided by the spider lily leaves.

Careful examination will show that many of the spider lily stalks that recently supported the blossoms now have mature seeds forming on them. There may be anywhere from one to ten such seeds on each flower stalk, and their combined weight tends to bend these stalks over toward the water surface. By the later part of this season mature seeds are dropping into the river, sinking to the bottom, and being moved along by the river current. Those that land in an appropriate location may germinate and become future members of the spider lily colony.

Other Summer Features

• *Great blue herons and great egrets have completed their annual nesting cycle at their rookeries. The adults and fully grown young return to the rapids to feed heavily on fish.*

• *Young bald eagles, recently fledged from nest sites along the river, actively feed with adult eagles, and can sometimes be seen landing on rocks in the rapids in search of fish.*

• *Anytime of day, but especially late in the afternoon, adult male bullfrogs hidden somewhere in the riverine landscape call across the river.*

• *Red-winged blackbirds continue to be active and vocal residents among the rapids.*

• *Dragonflies and damselflies patrol the air over the river in search of insect prey.*

• *Cicadas and katydids call from the trees along the riverbank.*

Autumn (September through November)

By September, some of this year's seed crop, recently dropped into the river, have germinated on substrates within the river that allow them to take hold, even if only temporarily. These seedlings are now sending their first new leaves above the water surface. This first sign of a potential new member of the spider lily colony is a single, narrow, green leaf extending 2 to 10 inches above the water surface. In most cases it is the product of a seed that has settled on a quiet, sandy-bottomed area within the rapids of the river where the water is only a few inches deep. There may be only a single plant, or there may be a dozen or more new seedlings that are trying to begin life in the same quiet sandy area. Other seeds may have landed in rock crevices and have a firmer foothold on their substrate.

The future survival of all of these seedlings depends on their being able to maintain their position against the rising currents of the river that will likely occur in the coming winter season. Meanwhile, as autumn progresses, the adult spider lilies and the young seedling plants lose their leaves and the scene at the river rapids again becomes one that is black and white, rather than green and lush. Winter has returned to the spider lily colony and to the river shoals where it lives.

Other Autumn Features

• *Newborn turtles hatch and enter the river from eggs deposited in spring.*

• *Fall colors progress among the riverside trees: sycamores and box elders provide light browns and yellows, tulip poplars bright yellows, sweet gums and black gums deep reds, river birch light yellows, red maples bright reds and yellows, and American beech golden browns.*

• *Winter bird migrants, including ruby and golden-crowned kinglets, dark-eyed juncos, and white-throated sparrows, feed in mixed flocks in the forests along the river.*

• *By November many life forms become less noticeable - songbirds are quiet, red-winged blackbirds abandon their nesting habitats in the shoals, and river cooters no longer bask on the rocks in the rapids.*

• *The cicadas and katydids are quiet.*

Where the Lilies Live

When considering most wildflowers, we tend to think of them growing in a seedbed that has rich, deep soil with some intermediate type of moisture and exposure to a good mixture of shade and sunlight. Maybe they are growing in a place we can walk through so we can examine the plants "up close and personal." Not so with the Rocky Shoals Spider Lily.

The seedbed of the Rocky Shoals Spider Lily is sandy deposits among cracks and crevices of rugged chunks of bedrock at the bottom of the Catawba River. Its roots and lower leaves are not only submerged, but are also constantly resisting the changing currents of the river as it swiftly flows across the bedrock shoals. Since most of the plants are in the middle of the river, they receive nearly full sunlight all day long. And, unless you canoe through these shoals, or are willing to wade in knee deep water over very slippery and jagged bedrock, you can not see these plants up close and personal. Rather, you will need to enjoy them from some distance away, maybe through binoculars, while you remain safely on the riverbank.

Preparation of the Rocky Shoals Spider Lily's seedbed has taken time – a great deal of time by our human standards. As the Catawba River flowed across the Piedmont landscape over the eons, it changed (and is changing) its own riverbed, banks and floodplain. In many areas, the river is cutting deeper into the riverbed by eroding the bedrock that forms the substrate or floor of the river. In some locations, it is depositing sediments and actually causing buildup of its riverbed. In the outside bends of the river it is eroding the riverbank cutting away soil and rock, while on the inside of river bends it is depositing sediments, building up the banks. Some of these changes, especially soil erosion, can be quite

Generalists vs. Specialists

In terms of their habitat requirements, wildflowers may be classified as generalists or specialists. Many species are generalists in that they can live under quite varied habitat conditions ranging from fields, woodland edges, roadsides, etc, and can grow in various soil types (the daisy might be an example of a generalist). By contrast, the Rocky Shoals Spider Lily is a specialist in that it has very distinct habitat requirements that are met only in the sandy crevices among the rugged ancient rocks of the shoals and rapids of a few large southeastern rivers. Conditions in all other habitat types, although suitable for many other plants, do not seem to meet the survival needs of this spider lily.

dramatic and readily observable. For instance, sediment deposits or losses following a major storm event may be very evident. However, changes in the river's bedrock substrate over time typically occur so extremely slowly that they are not apparent to people unless special measures are made to record them.

It is these changes in the river's bedrock that are important to the Rocky Shoals Spider Lilies. All bedrock erodes slowly under the constant flow of the river. In our Piedmont region we have a great diversity of bedrock types based on their structure and mineral composition. All of these Piedmont rock types are ancient (hundreds of millions of years old), and all erode, or weather, at different rates. As the Catawba River has flowed over these rock types it has cut

its bed to different depths. In areas where the rocks are most erodable the river bed is relatively deep and narrow, while in areas of more resistant bedrock the river is wider and shallower. Many of these wide, shallow areas form the shoals or rapids of today's river. Such rapids can be focal points for important things. It is here, at these wide shallow places, that much of human history has been written along the rivers. Here is where people could most readily cross rivers before the days of ferry boats or bridges, and in these shallows is where people could more easily catch fish to eat. Likewise, here is where herons, egrets, bald eagles, and other birds, frequently come to catch their fish. And here is where the Rocky Shoals Spider Lily finds the habitat conditions it needs for its survival.

Rocky Shoals Spider Lily Protected Status

The Rocky Shoals Spider lily is presently known to occur in nine rivers from Alabama's Cahaba River on the west to South Carolina's Catawba River on the east. In all three of the states where the Rocky Shoals Spider Lily occurs, it is considered to be in danger of extinction. Its "official" status in each state is: Alabama - Imperiled in the State; Georgia - Endangered; and South Carolina - Imperiled in the State.

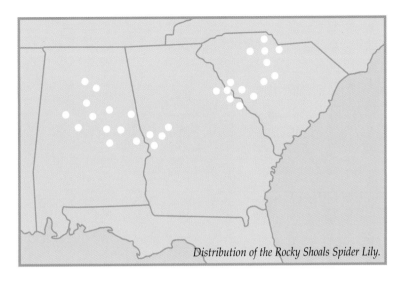

Distribution of the Rocky Shoals Spider Lily.

World Wide Distribution

This species was first recorded by William Bartram in May 1773 when he was traveling and recording native plants in the Carolinas, Georgia and Florida. In May of that year he was along the Savannah River near Augusta, Georgia. Here, after weeks in the field noting flowering plants of many kinds, he noted that "nothing in vegetable nature was more pleasing than the odoriferous pancratium fluitans (spider lilies) which almost alone possesses the rocky islets which just appear above the water." Bartram misclassified the spider lily, which was properly reclassified in later years and today has the scientific name Hymenocallis coronaria.

Dr. Larry Davenport of Samford University in Birmingham, Alabama has conducted the most extensive studies to date on the Rocky Shoals Spider Lily and is the authority on the distribution and other life history factors of this plant. He has noted that in addition to the special habitat requirements of a rocky stream bed, flowing water, and full sunlight, another apparent requirement of the spider lily is a subtropical climate. Thus, the spider lily is not found in large river rapids throughout the country. On the contrary, it is restricted to rapids of major southeastern rivers of Alabama, Georgia, and South Carolina. For the most part the lily is found in shoals where the rivers leave the Piedmont region and drop in elevation to the level of the coastal plain region

(the "fall line"). The Rocky Shoals Spider Lily is presently known to occur in nine rivers from Alabama's Cahaba River on the west to South Carolina's Catawba River on the east.

Undoubtedly, because of its special habitat requirements, this spider lily had a rather limited distribution even centuries ago. However, today it is even more restricted due in large part to the extensive construction of dams that occurred in the 20th century. These dams were constructed to form reservoirs and related facilities for power generation, flood control, and related functions. However, some of the dams and reservoirs also flooded or otherwise impacted shoals inhabited by the Rocky Shoals Spider Lily.

Altogether, Dr. Davenport estimates that there are approximately 60 populations of the spider lily. Some of these populations consist of only a few plants, while others consist of large expansive colonies. The two largest known colonies are those on our Catawba River at Landsford Canal State Park, and those on Alabama's Cahaba River (where the lily is called the Cahaba Lily).

The Fall Line: the area where rivers leave the Piedmont region and drop in elevation to the level of the coastal plain region.

The Catawba River

South Carolina Distribution

In South Carolina, the Rocky Shoals Spider Lily is known to occur in colonies among shoals of three major river systems: the Savannah River, the Broad River, and the Catawba River. Some of these "colonies" consist of only a few plants. The following information is largely summarized from data provided in the South Carolina Rare, Threatened, and Endangered Species Inventory as maintained by the SC Department of Natural Resources.

Savannah River

Colonies are known to occur in the main stem of the Savannah River and one of its tributaries. In Aiken County, in the area where Interstate 20 crosses the river, there are two colonies recorded in the rocky shoals of the river. This is the general location where William Bartram made the first recorded observation of this species in 1773. Next to the colony at Landsford Canal State Park, these colonies near I-20 on the Savannah River are the largest known colonies in South Carolina. Several miles upstream of Interstate 20 there is another colony in the Sumter National Forest area of the Savannah River. This colony has been noted to be growing in "muck" rather than among rocky shoals.

Further upriver in McCormick County there are several widely spaced colonies in Stevens Creek, a tributary of the Savannah River. All of these are recorded to be growing in rocky shoals.

Broad River

Three small colonies occur in rocky shoals and gravelly deposits of the Broad River system in the vicinity of Columbia in Richland County. One colony is about 2 miles upstream of I-20, and two colonies are near the confluence with the Saluda River. In fact, one of the latter colonies is just downstream of this confluence and is therefore technically in the Congaree River, which is the name that the river assumes after this confluence.

Two small colonies occur in the Broad River in extreme northwestern Richland County: one in Bookman Shoals, and the other at Freshley Shoals.

The most upstream colonies known to occur on the Broad River are at the town of Lockhart in Union County. Here two small colonies occur in rocky shoals of the river.

Catawba River

Four colonies are presently recognized.
• A small colony (recently discovered and not presently listed in the Rare, Threatened, Endangered Species Inventory) among rocky habitats at the upper end of Cedar Creek Reservoir (Stumpy Pond) on the Lancaster/Chester County

line is the most downstream colony known.
• A small colony occurs upstream of Highway 9, in Chester County, adjacent to Courtney Island.
• The largest known colony is in Chester/Lancaster Counties, at Landsford Canal State Park.
• The most upstream colony occurs among shoals in York County at the confluence of Sugar Creek with the Catawba River.

More about the Catawba River....

The Catawba River is one of a series of well known rivers of our Piedmont region that eventually join together to form the Santee River. The Catawba begins as a series of small mountain trout streams draining the southern face of the Blue Ridge Mountains in Burke, Caldwell, and McDowell Counties, North Carolina. When these streams come together at the foot of the mountains near Morganton in Burke County NC, they form the beginning of what we call the Catawba River. The Catawba then flows approximately 225 miles through the Piedmont of North Carolina and South Carolina. In Fairfield County, South Carolina, its name changes to the Wateree River.

Draining the mountainous country to the west of the Catawba River are the Broad River and, to its west, the Saluda River. These two major river systems flow south and join in Columbia to form the Congaree River. About 35 miles south of Columbia, the Congaree River joins the Wateree River to form the Santee River, which flows on to the ocean.

Of the rivers in the Santee system, the Catawba is the one most associated with the changes that have occurred in the Piedmont region of the Carolinas during the 20th century. The Catawba has been described as one of the country's most electrified rivers. Indeed, by 1930 Duke Power had constructed 10 reservoirs along the river, with an 11th and final reservoir (Lake Norman) being finished in 1959. These reservoirs provided for the generation of electricity that helped establish the basis for industry at a time when agriculture, the long term economic basis in the Catawba valley, was in sharp decline. Today, these reservoirs, dams, and power plants function daily to provide electricity, drinking water, flood control, sewage treatment water, recreation, and generally enhanced living conditions for millions of people living and working daily in our region.

Catawba-Wateree River System

One of the sections of the Catawba River that is not impounded and that still has much of its "free flowing" character is the 30 mile-long reach between the Lake Wylie Dam near Fort Mill/Rock Hill, and the headwaters of Fishing Creek Lake near Lancaster. Approximately 20 miles downstream of the Lake Wylie dam are the 2 mile-long shoals that are within Landsford Canal State Park. Here, in these shoals, among the free flowing waters, and near the growing and thriving towns and busy Interstate Highways of the Piedmont region of South Carolina, lives the world's largest known colony of the Rocky Shoals Spider Lily.

Landsford Canal State Park Distribution

At Landsford, the Rocky Shoals Spider Lily is said to "fill the rapids," but it really doesn't fill them all. In fact, when visitors begin their hike downstream along the rapids there is not a spider lily to be seen. Even after walking some distance there are still no spider lilies in view. It is only after a hike of about 0.75 miles, when visitors reach the spider lily overlook that they see "a rapids full of spider lilies." The question of why extensive areas of apparent suitable habitat for the lilies upstream and downstream of the colony remain unoccupied by the species is still to be answered. Suffice it to say that the present distribution of the Rocky Shoals Spider Lily in the rapids at Landsford is limited to certain areas.

In 2001, a University of North Carolina at Charlotte student, Jason Mann, worked to delineate the outline of the Rocky Shoals Spider Lily colony in the rapids at Landsford Canal State Park. With the use of Global Positioning System equipment he obtained the first accurate data on the distribu-tion of the spider lily at Landsford. More detailed and technical data are available for review by request through the office at Landsford Canal State Park.

Note: The history of the Santee River basin is a fascinating story of people, natural resources, and enterprise. This history is told in many places. One very readable volume is by Henry Savage Jr in his book, "River Of The Carolinas: The Santee." This book is one volume in the famous series of sixty-eight books written between 1938 and 1974 referred to as the "The Rivers Of America" series. Each book in the series provides a history of a major American river. The Santee volume was first published in 1956 and updated in 1968. Throughout, its contents either focus on the Catawba River or are otherwise very applicable to the Catawba River section of the Santee system. See the general references section at the back of this book.

Ecological Associates of the Rocky Shoals Spider Lily

The Rocky Shoals Spider Lilies thrive in the rapids at Landsford Canal State Park because these rocky rapids provide the specific habitat factors required by this particular plant species. The rapids also serve as habitat for many other forms of life that either need, or are otherwise attracted to, the unique conditions that occur there. Indeed, some of these other species not only live in the rapids with the spider lilies, they also directly or indirectly utilize the spider lilies as protective cover, nesting habitat, and possibly as a food source. Thus, the spider lilies not only use the rapids as habitat; they are themselves a functional part of this habitat.

This chapter provides additional information on some of these associates in hopes of providing the reader with a fuller appreciation of the diverse and interwoven relationships that occur among the plants and animals within these rapids at Landsford Canal State Park.

Note: The scientific names of the species described here, as well as all the plant and animals mentioned throughout the book, can be found in the Appendix.

What is an Ecological Associate? Plants or animals utilizing some of the same habitat.

Insects and other Invertebrates

The Catawba River rapids at Landsford Canal State Park, like many river systems, provide habitat for a tremendous number of species of larval and adult insects ranging in size from tiny midge flies (frequently referred to as "no-see-ums") to dragon flies and other larger flying insects. When the Rocky Shoals Spider Lilies are leafed out, and when they are in flower, they become a part of the ecology of certain insect species, providing cover and resting places for adult insects, and providing food in the form of nectar and pollen to other species. In turn, some of these species provide pollination services for the spider lily as a means for it to produce seeds.

Dragonflies - Also known as "meadow hawks" and "skimmers," these 2-inch-long flying predators are common around rivers, ponds, and wet meadows. The adults fly over the Catawba River rapids and through the spider lily colony in search of small flying insects upon which they feed. Sometimes they perch on spider lily leaves and wait for small insects to fly close enough for them to fly out and capture. Females lay eggs in the river, which hatch into predaceous nymphs that inhabit quiet areas in the river. In spring nymphs crawl up onto spider lily leaves or other above water structures and transform into the flying adults.

Damselflies - These relatives of dragonflies can be readily distinguished from the latter when at rest because their wings fold upward. (Dragonfly wings are straight-out to their sides when they are at rest.) Also known as "snake doctors," damselflies are predatory and feed on small flying insects.

Damselflies are relatively weak fliers. Like dragonflies, they are active during daylight hours and are commonly observed within and over the spider lily colony.

Sphinx Moths - Sphinx moths are also known as "hawk moths" or "hummingbird moths." The latter name comes from their flying habits which are not the random flapping flight of most moths, but rather the rapid directional flight of a hummingbird. Some have 5-inch wingspans, and can fly over 30 miles per hour. Sphinx moths have large eyes, a long proboscis that allows them to extract nectar from tubular flowers, and pointed wings. Sphinx moths have been observed visiting newly opened spider lily flowers in the hours just after dark, and are thought to be one of the pollinators of the spider lilies.

Mayflies, Stoneflies, and Caddis Flies - Mayflies (600+ species), stoneflies (500+ species), and caddis flies (1,300 species) are groups of insects that are common in most bodies of higher quality water. They all lay their eggs in the water. Eggs hatch into larvae that go through several stages of development before they come to the water surface and transform into winged adults. As larvae, all of these species are important food for fish. Sometimes large numbers of individuals of mayflies or caddis flies transform into adults at the same time, resulting in a dense "hatch" that can form clouds of flying insects over the river surface. At these times, the leaves of the spider lilies, water willows and other vegetation can be covered with adults of these insects. Here these insects become important food items for the red-winged blackbirds that patrol the spider lily leaves looking for insects as food for both themselves and their new-born young waiting in nearby nests.

Fish

The rapids at Landsford Canal support a diverse and abundant fish community. Fishes common to many types of habitats (lakes, farm ponds, streams) occur here including some of our more prized gamefish such as largemouth bass, bluegill, redbreast sunfish, and channel catfish. In early springtime, white bass and striped bass up to ten pounds in size migrate through the rapids during their upstream "spawning runs." However, there is also an assemblage of smaller-sized species that occur in the rapids. These smaller "river species" include the following:

Snail Bullhead - one of the most common fish found in the shoals habitat is the snail bullhead. It occupies warm, medium to large rivers and favors high gradient, rocky sections. This small catfish, which rarely exceeds ten inches in total length, feeds mainly on insect larvae, snails, fish, and plant materials. Like other bullheads, the snail bullhead is fun to catch, and good to eat, and is often seen on an angler's stringer.

Spottail Shiner - this fish is common in running waters and is found in a variety of habitats, from soft, sandy bottoms to rocky, moderate gradient streams. One of the largest "minnows," it can reach six inches in total length. It feeds on small insects, mollusks such as the Asiatic clam, and plant material. The spottail shiner is an important source of food for gamefish.

Tesselated Darter - this member of the perch family is one of many species that have evolved specialized adaptations for living in flowing waters. Their body shapes are generally round, their pelvic fins are usually modified, and their swim bladders are lacking or poorly developed. These features help this species to live on the bottom in fast flowing waters. Eggs are laid in nests beneath rocks so they are not swept away in the current. This small fish seldom exceeds three inches in total length. Food items include immature insects and other small invertebrates such as midge larvae.

Birds

Much of "the action" observed at the overlook among the lilies is provided by bird species. Species that nest and feed among the lilies, or that feed in the river rapids around the lilies, are frequently seen flying back and forth among the lilies and over the rapids as they seek food for themselves and for their young in nests among the lily leaves or in trees along the river banks. Some of the species readily observed in the rapids or in the trees immediately along the river's edge include the following:

Bald Eagle - The Catawba River corridor provides important habitat for nesting bald eagles. This majestic nationally threatened bird can be seen perched in the top of a riverside tree or in flight while searching the rocky shoals for prey. Its diet consists mainly of fish, particularly catfish, but also occasional water birds and small mammals. The bald eagle requires large pines and suitable food resources for nesting, such as that found around Landsford Canal State Park. The snow-white head and tail of the adult is distinctive.

Osprey - Sometimes called fish hawk, the osprey is a fairly common resident along the Catawba River. Birds are particularly prevalent during spring and fall migration, but occur in summer as well and nest here. The osprey is a superb fisher and fish comprise its entire diet. Birds may be seen hovering over a potential catch or diving from significant heights to nab their prey. The osprey's strong, curved talons and rough-padded feet are well adapted for catching and grasping slippery fish. They in turn are sometimes attacked by bald eagles, forcing them to give up their meal to the larger bird.

Great Blue Heron - This familiar long-legged wader occurs as a winter resident and late summer visitor. Birds are usually found patiently stalking prey in the shallows or shoals of the river. Its long flexible neck and sharp spear-like bill is used to strike unwary fish and other aquatic animals such as frogs and salamanders. The great blue is our largest heron, standing nearly four feet tall. Nesting birds generally occur more towards the coast in heavy-timbered swamps and river bottomlands.

Great Egret - This large white wader occurs in the upstate region in late summer and early fall as a post-breeding disperser. At this time, birds may be seen searching the shallow waters and shoals of the river for fish that constitute a large portion of their diet. The great egret is a well-known symbol of bird conservation. This species was nearly driven to extinction by 19th-Century plume hunters. Successful conservation efforts in the early 20th Century brought this bird back from the brink and today this beautiful species is a fairly common part of South Carolina's avifauna. The great egret can be distinguished from other white herons by its larger size, black legs and yellow bill.

Canada Goose - Prior to the 1970s, Canada geese were considered migratory waterfowl in South Carolina and were not known to nest here. Over the years, their numbers steadily declined. State wildlife officials reacted by initiating a goose re-stocking program that was so successful that the bird became well established by the early 1980s. These birds readily accepted their new home and quickly became naturalized. Many abandoned their natural tendency to migrate and thus established themselves as nesting residents. Today, the Canada goose is a common bird in many areas of upstate South Carolina including the Catawba River corridor. Pairs or groups of these handsome-looking geese are occasionally sighted from Landsford Canal State Park.

Turkey Vulture – Recent scientific studies have changed the way we view this American vulture. Once classified as a bird of prey, the turkey vulture is now thought to be more closely related to storks and flamingos or scavengers. It is a common resident of the Catawba River region, spending much of its time soaring aloft on dihedral wings. Its keen sense of smell and sight enables it to readily locate its primary

food source -- carrion. At close range, this vulture is easily recognized by its large blackish-brown body and unfeathered red head, which is an adaptation for feeding on carrion. The turkey vulture is a social bird, often occurring in large communal roosts. It is a short-distance migrant in the northern parts of its range.

Prothonotary Warbler - The Catawba River shoreline provides ideal nesting habitat for this brilliantly colored wood warbler. The prothonotary warbler typically occurs as a coastal plain bird, although its population extends inland along several South Carolina rivers including the Catawba. In the spring, its loud ringing song is a commonly heard sound while canoeing or while walking the trails at Landsford. An interesting aspect of this species' natural history is that it is one of only two North American wood warblers that nests in natural cavities. The prothonotary warbler is easily recognized by its striking golden-yellow plumage and blue-gray wings.

Red-winged Blackbird - The male red-winged blackbird is easily recognized by its red epaulets or wing patches. It is a common year-round resident of the Catawba River corridor. During spring and early summer, this species occurs in stands of spider lilies, which they use for nesting. The nest, which typically contains three to five eggs, is built of weed stems and grasses. At Landsford, we have observed that the birds also use parts of the spider lily flowers in nest construction. All of these materials are woven by the birds and secured to the spider lily stalks, directly over open water. Territorial males frequently perch among the flower clusters while singing, thus providing a beautiful contrast of black and white to the observer.

Did you know….. Over 120 different species of birds have been spotted in the Landsford Canal State Park area?

Reptiles and Amphibians

There are many species of amphibians and reptiles that live in the habitat types found within Landsford Canal State Park. Those most likely to be observed in the Catawba River rapids, and in association with the spider lilies, include the following.

Bullfrog - This is the largest species of frog in this area of South Carolina. Individuals inhabit the river banks and the islands within the river. Their "jug-o-rum" calls can sometimes be heard over the sound of the river rapids in the area of the spider lilies. Adult bullfrogs are voracious predators, eating insects of many kinds, but also eating other frogs, snakes, and even small birds.

River Cooter - This species of turtle prefers the flowing waters of large rivers and is the turtle most frequently observed sunning on the rocks in the rapids at Landsford. Sometimes large numbers of these turtles will congregate on the same rock or log to bask in the sun. They spend most of their adult life in the river, and feed largely on plant materials and invertebrate animals. However, female river cooters come ashore in large numbers in late spring to dig nests and lay eggs in the riparian habitats along the river. Many of these nests are robbed by mammalian predators as evidenced by the broken egg shells found around the opened nests. The eggs hatch by late summer and baby turtles make their way to the river.

Common Snapping Turtle - Unlike the River Cooter, which spends much of its time basking on rocks and logs, snapping turtles are rarely seen. There are plenty of them here in the rapids, but because they rarely bask, they are seldom observed by visitors. Snapping turtles spend much of their time patrolling the bottom of the river in search of food which consists largely of fish and other forms of animal life. Snapping turtles grow to over 25 lbs. (NOTE: A 55-pound common snapper was recently captured near Davidson, NC.)

Brown Water Snake

Water Snakes

There are four species of harmless water snakes that inhabit the rapids in the area of the spider lilies. These are the northern water snake, the brown water snake, the red-bellied water snake, and the queen snake. Of these four, the northern and brown water snakes are the most abundant in the rapids at Landsford Canal State Park. Both of these species are largely fish eaters and they find much to feed on among the dense fish populations in the rapids.

Mammals

Most of our species of mammals are largely active at night, in the very early morning, or late evening hours. Therefore, they are not readily observable by visitors to the spider lily overlook. There are many species that inhabit the river bank areas of the rapids, and the two species discussed below commonly move about in the rapids in the area of the spider lilies.

Beaver - The largest rodent species native to North America, beavers can weigh up to 60 pounds and grow to over 45 inches in total length. Their signs are abundant along the shoreline at the rapids in the form of cut tree stumps, but they themselves are rarely seen. They eat plants, but fortunately they do not seem to noticeably impact the Spider Lilies.

Muskrat - Like the beaver, the muskrat is an aquatic rodent that makes a good living in the Catawba River, including in the rapids at Landsford Canal State Park. Muskrats are small compared to beavers. While they may reach up to 2 ft in total length, adults typically weigh less than 3 lbs. Muskrats, like

beavers, are largely nocturnal. However, their signs are common among the rapids of the river, including den entrances, caches of freshwater clam shells, and footprints in the mud along the shoreline.

Raccoon – The raccoon is a common species of mammal that finds an abundance of food in the shallows of the Landsford rapids. Raccoons are animals of the forest that spend much of the daytime resting in hollow logs or in holes of standing dead trees. At dusk, they emerge and spend much of the night actively searching for food. The river provides various food sources for raccoons, including crayfish, and freshwater clams, that it gathers in the shallow rocky habitats of the shoals. Their footprints can frequently be seen in muddy areas of the riverbank.

Note: Several close relatives of the spider lily are toxic to animals, and the spider lily may also be toxic or at least distasteful. Partially eaten bulbs of spider lilies have been found lying on the river bottom in the rapids, as if an animal, such as a beaver, pulled it loose from the rocks, took a couple of bites from it, found it distasteful, and dropped it.

Other Plant Species

    The rather harsh conditions of the rapids at Landsford Canal State Park provide habitat for the Rocky Shoals Spider Lily, but for few other plants. Most species are not adapted to live here. Their seeds may land in the river, but the river, its rocky substrate, and its ever changing currents make it inhospitable to most species of native vegetation. However, the visitor at the spider lily overlook will notice a few other species growing in the rapids, including the following:

Water Willow - Water willow shares the rocky/sandy areas of the rapids with the spider lilies, and is probably the lily's most abundant botanical associate. Their slender stems, with light green willow-shaped leaves, contrast strongly with the dark green, strap-like leaves of the spider lilies. Water willow flowers from May through summer. The blueish flowers are about 1 inch wide and consist of several lobes and a lower lip. They are quite intricate, and pretty, but lack the large and showy features of the spider lilies. Whereas the spider lily flowers can be seen from a considerable distance, the flowers of its associate, water willow, need close inspection to be appreciated.

Black Willow - These are small trees that grow in wet sunny areas. They are typically abundant on pond margins, river banks, and similar locations. At Landsford they are a common plant on the edges of many of the small islands within the rapids. Thus, while they are typically not in the watery habitats of the spider lily, they can be seen in the mid-rapids areas where there is enough soil on small islands. They can tolerate being submerged part of the time.

Cardinal Flower - There are a number of native wildflowers that inhabit the higher and sunny ground of the small islets that dot the rapids within the areas of the spider lily colony. One of the showy members of this group is cardinal flower, so named for its bright red stalk of late summer flowers. Like most red-colored flowers, cardinal flower is a favorite of hummingbirds. It blooms on the islets among the lilies, and in sunny locations along the immediate bank of the river. Some other showy flower associates of cardinal flower in late summer are Joe Pye Weed, seedbox, and blue lobelias.

Visiting the Lilies at Landsford Canal State Park

The spider lilies are available for public viewing and enjoyment at Landsford Canal State Park throughout their blooming season as well as other times of the year. In order to experience them "at their very best" we suggest you visit the park during the peak season of blooming which typically occurs between mid May and early June.

Traveling To Landsford Canal State Park

Landsford Canal State Park's main entrance, located in Chester County, SC, is reached from Highway 21. Traveling north on Hwy 21 go 8 miles north of its intersection with Hwy 9, then turn right onto County Rd 327. Traveling south on Hwy 21 from the Rock Hill area, you will find County Rd 327 to be 16 miles south of I-77. Once you have turned onto County Rd 327 travel 2 miles to the park's main entrance on your left. Take the park entrance road 1 mile to the parking areas. At this point you have arrived at the park's office area. There are restroom facilities and information brochures available here.

The Foot Trails

From the main parking area (park office area) of Landsford Canal State Park you will have a hike of approximately 0.75 miles to the lily colony and its overlook area. Foot trails providing scenic views and historical information take you downstream to the overlook area. One of the

trails (The Nature Trail) leads along the Catawba River and provides very nice views of the river and the upper portions of its Landsford rapids (there are no lilies at this point in the rapids), while the other trail (The Canal Trail) leads along the historic canal for which the park is named. You have the option of walking one trail down river to the lilies, and returning by the other trail.

These trails traverse the rather flat floodplain area of the river and the historic canal tow path, and thus provide rather easy walking for visitors. However, these are woodland trails, and do contain the normal items typically encountered on such trails from tree roots to some areas of uneven ground. There are also some areas where a short series of steps are constructed to assist hikers over small impediments.

The Overlook : What You'll See

The Spider Lily Overlook is a cleared area along the bank of the river that provides good views of the lilies. Here you will have a grand view of the expansive rapids in that part of the river, and during peak blooming season (mid-May to early June) you will be presented with one of the grandest natural history sights in the Southeast. The very core of the largest known colony of the Rocky Shoals Spider Lily will be before you across the wide and rushing river.

The flowers are in the open part of the river, and not immediately next to the river bank. Thus, you may not have a chance to view them on an up-close basis. However, if you bring a pair of binoculars you will be able to see more details about individual flowers. Either way, with or without binoculars, you will not feel at all disappointed if you take the time to make this hike to see the lilies during their peak blooming season.

In addition to binoculars, we suggest you also consider bringing a camera. Photo opportunities of the colony are quite good from the Lily Overlook.

Canoeing to The Lilies

In addition to hiking to the lilies, as described above, visitors can also canoe or kayak to the lilies. Visitors can launch canoes/kayaks at the park office area and travel downstream to the lily colony. A take-out is available at the lower end of the park, downstream of the lily colony. However, because of navigational and safety considerations, you should not attempt this boat trip until you have discussed your plans with the park staff. Better yet, make your first trip with the park staff on one of the guided canoe trips that they provide at various times of the year. Contact park personnel about these canoe trips. *(See Sources of Additional Information in the Appendix.)*

Lily Fest

If you have not experienced the Rocky Shoals Spider Lily, but you have an interest in: seeing it in peak blooming season; hearing about the lilies from local biologists; learning more about the park and its history; or, hearing about other natural features of the river and the park, then you should consider attending Lily Fest as your introduction to the spider lilies and to Landsford Canal State Park. Lily Fest is an annual celebration of the lilies that occurs on a Sunday afternoon in the middle part of May (call the park at 803.789.5800 for details).

On this day the park staff, other employees of the State Park Service, volunteers from the Katawba Valley Land Trust, the South Carolina Wildlife Federation, the Friends of Landsford and other groups, work together to provide a fun and educational event for the public. There will be more visitors in the park on this day than any other, but that is part of the fun of the event - people of all ages making the annual pilgrimage to the rapids at Landsford Canal State Park to see this annual and unique natural history occurrence in their river.

Part of the historic Landsford Canal this lifting lock was an important feature of the canal. Built from a design that dates from the sixteenth century, the locks of Landsford allowed boats to overcome a thirty-six foot fall in elevation without danger of traveling through the shoals of the river.

Park History

The State Park at Landsford Canal was created in 1970 when Duke Energy donated approximately 200 acres to the State of South Carolina to preserve the historic canal that allowed cotton boats to bypass the 2-mile long series of rapids in this area of the river. It was after the establishment of this new state park that the conservation community learned about the presence of the Rocky Shoals Spider Lilies in the rapids. Over the years, their status as a rare species has become recognized and their popularity with the general public has increased.

In recent years, Landsford Canal State Park and adjoining public conservation lands have been expanded through the efforts of the Katawba Valley Land Trust working in partnership with the SC Department of Parks, Recreation, and Tourism, the South Carolina Department of Natural Resources, and Crescent Resources, LLC (a Duke Energy Company). Crescent offered the land to the Katawba Valley Land Trust and worked cooperatively to make sales of the land compatible with Katawba Valley Land Trust schedules.

One of these land expansions has added over 1000 acres of public lands adjacent to the 448-acre state park. This expansion of public holdings protects major natural and cultural resources associated with the Landsford Canal area,

Landsford Canal State Park is open Thursday through Monday (closed on Tuesdays and Wednesdays). Landsford is a day-use park; there are no camping areas. Park hours are 9am to 6pm. The park staff offers programs related to the Spider Lilies, the river, the historic canal, and other natural and cultural features of the park. They also offer canoe trips through the rapids during select weeks in spring and autumn months. To learn about these programs, check on daily operating hours for the park, reserve the picnic shelter, check on the status of the spider lilies (blooming season, etc), and to get the planned date for Lily Fest, call the park office at 803-789-5800. To obtain a copy of the park brochure you can write to the staff at: Manager, Landsford Canal State Park, 2051 Park Drive, Catawba, SC 29704. There is currently at $2.00 per person entrance fee to the park.

and provides an important buffer area for the Rocky Shoals Spider Lily colony in the Landsford rapids. It is managed by SC DNR.

The Year of the Rains: Spring 2003

The late 1990s and the early years of the new century had been marked by a prolonged drought in the Catawba River basin. The situation became so extreme by mid 2002 that record-setting low-flow river conditions occurred within the basin and special water conservation regulations were put in place in some locations. The drought created problems for municipal and state officials, for Duke Energy operations personnel and for many river recreationists.

However, one specific item the drought did not impact was the viewing of the spider lilies in the rapids at Landsford Canal State Park. In fact, during the drought years, it was largely taken for granted that the lilies could be seen in their full glory any time during their blooming season. As park personnel, KVLT and other partners planned for Lily Fest (the park's celebration of the lilies conducted each spring) during the drought years, we might have worried about such things as the day's weather, if many people would attend or if the eagles would show up at their nest. We never worried about the reliable, fine display of the lilies. All that changed in the spring of 2003.

Weather forecasters predicted that the drought conditions might begin to break before the end of 2002, and by late autumn the river valley did begin to get some extended precipitation. Then, as the winter and early spring of 2003 progressed, we unofficially went from drought conditions to normal rain, to above-normal rain to prolonged deluge. Rainfall for the first six months in 2003 was reported at 36.98 inches by the weather station in Charlotte. The average for that time period is usually 21.97 inches. We had received close to a year's worth of precipitation (approximately 45 inches) in the first six months.

The impacts of this extensive precipitation were many. Most importantly the Catawba River reservoirs returned to full pond elevation for the first time in a long time, restoring our region's water supply for drinking, sewage treatment and the generation of electricity, among other things. On the natural history front, the extensive winter and early spring rains filled and maintained the riparian wetlands along the Catawba River for the first time in several years. During the drought years, there was very little reproduction by salamander species due to lack of sustained water in their pools. The year of the rains, however, had been a banner year for them.

Other natural history impacts involved the river itself. On several occasions, the river came out of its banks and flowed through the adjacent forests. The results were that all the leaf litter in these areas had been swept away and a line of leaves and twigs rested at the high water mark, much like sea weed and other natural materials on the beach mark the highest tide. New whitish sand deposits are readily visible in the woods where the river waters deposited them during its high flows.

Through the end of June, the flow in the river varied from "high" to "very high," and weeks went by with no rocks being visible in the rapids due to the high river levels.

Flow rates in excess of 10,000 cubic feet per second (cfs) were common, with several periods over 20,000 cfs. At approximately 13,000 cfs, the river is considered "bank full" at the park. During the higher flows, water filled Landsford Canal itself to the top of its banks, rushing through the canal in a frightening torrent. Flows like this had not been seen in recent years. (Today, flows of this level at Landsford Canal are notable). However, it is likely that

floods of much greater intensity occurred with some routine frequency prior to the establishment of the dams.

Wildlife along the river had to adjust in various ways. During the higher flows, river otters were observed "playing" on the nature trail (then under water), in a location where they would normally not occur. The numerous turtles that typically bask on exposed rocks in the river had no exposed rocks for weeks at a time. Many of these turtles were observed basking on tree roots along the river bank as they sought substitutes for their unavailable river rocks. Today visitors can observe caches of empty clam shells well up in the forest and may wonder how they got there. The answer – this is where the muskrat had his dinner, at the water's edge, when the river was in flood stage.

And what of the spider lilies? How has the high water affected them? Lily Fest 2003 was scheduled for Sunday May 18. In early May, a group of volunteers who would assist at Lily Fest met with Park Manager Al James and Park Ranger Don Oneppo to make plans. A concern at that time was the blooming of the lilies. By this time of year, lily leaves frequently extend several feet above water level, and the first flowers are opening. In 2003, the water remained so high that there were no signs of the lily plants at all. We wondered if they were still there, if they were growing.

About 10 days before Lily Fest, the water dropped slightly and Al was able to take some photographs of the lily colony area. The very tops of the lily plants were exposed. Al's photos showed that the lilies had grown under the water and even flowered, but the stems and flowers were severely damaged. The river flow was thrashing the plants about and ripping the flowers to pieces. Soon Al and Don began to receive messages that large masses of lilies were washing up on shorelines in downstream reservoirs, indicating that the high river flows were uprooting some of the plants. This was the situation prior to Lily Fest. The local media were informed and they advised the public that there would be few lilies to view this year.

On Lily Fest day, things remained largely unchanged. The weather was unseasonably cold and cloudy. Even so, volunteers were there to work and greet the public, but the lilies, as predicted, were not. The river flow was still very high due to continuing rain events, and only the tops of very tattered spider lily plants and few flowers were visible.

As May turned into June, conditions remained unchanged. Al and Don were brought many more clusters of spider lily plants that had been dislodged from the river bottom and floated downstream. These plants were placed in plastic pools at the edge of the forest behind their office.

Several interesting sidelight observations were made from these plants and helped compensate somewhat for the lack of a "good lily viewing season." The first new observation was that the spider lily bulb clusters were full of crayfish, which soon came out and filled the plastic pools. Apparently providing habitat for crayfish and other invertebrates is another ecological function of the lilies during their lives in the rapids. An even more interesting observation was that the leaves of these lilies kept in the plastic pools were quickly, and completely, eaten by deer. Unlike in nature, where the lily leaves are in mid river and not available to the deer, these lilies were in pools beside the forest. The deer simply walked up and ate with no inconvenience. Thus, an important benefit the lilies may receive by living in the harsh environment of the rapids is protection from browsing deer, which do not wade into the swift water to feed on the lilies.

Then on Friday, June 27, 2003, Al James informed us that the river flow was finally down and the rocks in the rapids exposed for the first time this year. On the morning of Sunday, June 29, several KVLT members walked to the spider lily overlook to get the first good view of the lilies this year, and to observe their condition after months of being submerged in high, swift water. What we found was exciting. Bright green spider lily plants stood erect among the rocks of the river and hundreds, maybe more than one thousand, beautiful flowers were in bloom. It wasn't nearly as spectacular as a typical Lily Fest day might look, but, because of the conditions experienced this spring, the sight that met our eyes was elating. It was obvious that some of the lily clusters were missing (due to being scoured out by the flood water), and it was noted that the water willow plants that normally grow with the lilies were not in evidence due to the floods.

Another impact of the prolonged high water became obvious about this same time. It was the near absence of the red-winged blackbirds over the river. These colorful and highly vocal birds typically nest among the lily leaves (as well as other locations), even using lily flowers as part of their nest construction. They are usually in abundance in the lily colony at this time of year, and give it a voice through the constant calling of the male birds. This year, with the lily leaves under water much of the spring; there were no nests in the colony.

These changes were obvious to us, a group of "experienced lily watchers." But the beauty of the lily, even in its damaged condition, still impresses the novice. As we stood there at the overlook, a couple of new visitors arrived and marveled at the abundant white blanket of flowers.

Lindsay Pettus, President of the KVLT, was with us this day to see the lilies. Looking out on the now rejuvenating lily colony that dominated the setting and bolstered our spirits, he noted that "surely next year these plants and the public will return stronger than ever."

And so they shall every year. The cardinal flowers will appear along the river bank and provide late summer nectar for the hummingbirds. The beauty berries will set their lavender colored berries along the trail in the fall, and the tree leaves will turn their magical fall color. Large flocks of winter songbirds will arrive from the north, and with squirrels, deer, and wild turkeys, partake of the abundant berries, acorns, hickory nuts, and beech nuts that the park vegetation has produced partially as a result of this year's abundant rain. In January, the bald eagles will begin nesting again at Landsford Canal, and in April the spring wildflowers will light up the nature trail. All this before the next Lily Fest, and all during this time the great Catawba River, with the water that nature provides, will roll on.

Preserving the Lilies at Landsford Canal State Park

It is the vision of the Katawba Valley Land Trust, and its partners, to acquire or otherwise preserve natural, cultural, and scenic resources of the Landsford Canal area and to make them available to the public for recreational and educational activities in ways that are compatible with their long-term protection. We hope that this booklet will be a contribution toward those goals.

Consistent with that objective, we ask that you please be aware of the following guidelines when visiting Landsford Canal State Park to observe the spider lilies.

• Observe the lilies from the shoreline overlook area, or on a park-led canoe trip. Wading out into the river from the Overlook area is strongly discouraged. The rocks in the river are extremely slippery and can result in a fall.

• If you do canoe the Landsford rapids and travel among the lilies, it is fun to stop and view them up close. However, please resist picking flowers. They will not hold their shape very long, and thus do not make a good "take home item." And please do not try to pull the plants up to transplant in your yard (or pool in your yard). The open rapids of the river provide the only effective habitat for this species of spider lily. However, there are cultivated spider lilies that will do well in gardens, and you might inquire about them at your local garden center.

If we all will take proper care of the Rocky Shoals Spider Lilies at Landsford Canal State Park, they, in their way, will help take care of us. As noted in the earlier in this book, the spider lilies at Landsford serve as a way to help many of our citizens become aware of the Catawba River and many of its other values that serve wildlife and people. The longer these flowers prosper at Landsford Canal, the more people will have a chance to discover them and recognize the need to ensure that the river continues to serve all who depend on it.

General References

1. River of the Carolinas: The Santee. Henry Savage Jr. The University Of North Carolina Press, Chapel Hill. 1968. 435 pp.

2. A Portrait of the Cahaba Lily. Jennifer Greer. Know Alabama.

3. The Captivating Cahaba. Shannon Haddock. Alabama Wildlife Federation. Spring 1999.

4. The Cahaba Lily: Its Distribution and Status in Alabama. L. J. Davenport. Journal Of Alabama Academy of Science. Vol. 67, No 4. October, 1996.

Sources of Additional Information

General status of the Rocky Shoals Spider Lily:
   South Carolina Department of Natural Resources
   Heritage Trust Section
   PO Box 167
   Columbia SC 29202.

Landsford Canal State Park, Lily Fest, and the Rocky Shoals Spider Lilies in the Catawba River rapids:
   Landsford Canal State Park
   2051 Park Drive
   Catawba , SC 29704
   Phone: 803- 789-5800

Other South Carolina State Parks:
   South Carolina Department of Parks, Recreation, and Tourism
   1205 Pendleton St
   Columbia, SC 29201

This book and land conservation along the Catawba River:
   Katawba Valley Land Trust
   PO Box 1776
   Lancaster, SC 29721-1776
   Phone: 803-285-9455

Appendix

List of common and scientific names of plants and animals mentioned in the text.

Plants

Trees:
American Beech (Fagus grandifolia)
Black Gum (Nyssa sylvatica)
Box Elder (Acer negundo)
Red Maple (Acer rubrum)
River Birch (Betula nigra)
Sweet Gum (Liquidambar styraciflua)
Sycamore (Platanus occidentalis)
Tulip Poplar, or Yellow Poplar (Liriodendron tulipifera)

Wildflowers (Herbs):
Atamasco Lily (Zephyranthes atamasco)
Black Willow (Salix nigra)
Cardinal Flower (Lobelia cardinalis)
Daffodil (Narcissus sp.)
Daisy (Chrysanthemum leucanthemum)
Fire Pink (Silene virginica)
Rocky Shoals Spider Lily (Hymenocallis coronaria)
Water Willow (Justicia americana)
Yellow Stargrass (Hypoxis hirsuta)

Animals

Invertebrates:
Caddisfly (Order: Trichoptera)
Damsel Fly (Order: Odonata)
Dragon Fly (Order: Odonata)
Cicada (Order: Homoptera)
Katydid (Order: Orthoptera)
Mayfly (Ephemeroptera)
Sphinx Moth (Order: Lepidoptera)
Stonefly (Order: Plecoptera)

Fishes:
Largemouth Bass (Micropterus salmoides)
Redbreast sunfish (Lepomis auritus)
Snail Bullhead (Ictalurus brunneus)
Spottail Shiner (Notropis hudsonius)
Tesselated Darter (Etheostoma olmstedi)

Amphibians:
Bullfrog (Rana catesbeiana)

Reptiles:
Brown Water Snake (Nerodia taxispilota)
River Cooter Turtles (Pseudemys concinna)
Common Snapping Turtle (Chelydra serpentina)
Musk Turtle (Sternotherus odoratus)
Northern Water Snake (Nerodia sipedon)
Queen Snake (Regina septemvittata)
Red-bellied Water Snake (Nerodia erythrogaster)

Birds:
Bald Eagle (Haliaeetus leucocephalus)
Black Vulture (Coragyps atratus)
Canada Goose (Branta canadensis)
Great Blue Heron (Ardea herodias)
Great Egret (Casmerodius albus)
Golden-crowned Kinglet (Regulus satrapa)
Osprey (Pandion haliaetus)
Protonotary Warbler (Protonotaria citrea)
Red-winged Blackbird (Agelaius phoeniceus)
Ruby-crowned Kinglet (Regulus calendula)
Slate-colored Junco (Junco hyemalis)
Turkey Vulture (Cathartes aura)

Mammals:
Beaver (Castor canadensis)
Muskrat (Ondatra ziibethicus)
Raccoon (Procyon lotor)